science & song
for kids!

SING FOR THE EARTH

littlewild ANIMALS

claudia robin gunn

science: MELISSA R GUNN
illustrations: ELISE DE SILVA

Title: Science and Song – Sing for the Earth
Little Wild Animals
Copyright ©2025 by C Gunn & M Gunn/
Little Wild Music
Published by Little Wild Music
Authors: Songwriting by Claudia Robin Gunn
Science Notes & Activity Ideas by Melissa R Gunn
Illustrations by Elise De Silva
Book Design by Melissa R Gunn
Graphic Design by Claudia Robin Gunn
Audio Production by Tom Fox
All songs from the album Sing for the Earth – Little Wild Animals (2022) All rights reserved.

No part of this book may be reproduced in any form or by any means, electronic or mechanical, without permission in writing from the publisher Little Wild Music. Please contact Little Wild Music in the first instance for any requests regarding licensing, recording, performances, education, workshops etc.
(claudia@littlewildmusic.com)

ISBN Softcover POD 978-1-0670517-0-9
ISBN Hardcover POD 978-1-0670517-1-6
ISBN PDF 978-0-473-65342-2
ISBN Epub 978-0-473-65340-8

Proudly supported by Creative New Zealand

science & song

Songs are a great way to inspire curiosity. This book of science and songs puts a spotlight on conservation themes through a cast of animal characters from around the world with a special focus on Aotearoa.

Kiwi sisters Claudia and Melissa plus artist Elise De Silva invite kids to explore their wild side. Claudia's imaginative song lyrics are paired with fascinating facts and fun activity ideas written by Melissa. Playful original art by Elise enlivens the text. Claudia Gunn is an award-winning songwriter for kids and Melissa Gunn (PhD) is a science communicator and author.

These original tunes celebrate children's connection to the land and the animals that inhabit this planet around us. The notes are intended as a starting point for families and educators to stimulate further curious exploration.

On the recordings, Echidna Lullaby features Angie Who (Sydney), while Love Birds Love and Zoo Hullaballoo feature Christchurch duos Itty Bitty Beats and Loopy Tunes Preschool Music. Claudia and Melissa's mother Denise Gunn lends her harmonies to Loopy the Inchworm and Roly Poly Polar Bear.

This book uses a dyslexia-friendly font for increased accessibility.

Scan the QR code on this page to choose how and where to listen to the songs - available on streaming services and for download.

Use the labelled leaves to quickly find lyrics, activities or fun facts.

Our planet is full of a dazzling array of wild life — one of our earliest memories is watching David Attenborough's Our World on a very small television with our sisters. Having our own children, we found that kids relate to animals on an almost mystical level. We would meet together with our babies in prams and then they became toddlers running wild, and then bigger school kids taking an interest in all the stories and facts to discover, at the Auckland Zoo for real live animals, and the Auckland Museum for fascinating specimens and displays.

These hubs between our far flung houses were our favourite meeting points in places of wonder. So the songs in this songbook have been inspired both by those playful days, and in response to our children's concern and desire to take action on climate change and biodiversity loss.

We hope that these songs help kids find some fun as well as learn more about ecosystems and incredible creatures from Aotearoa and around the world. We invite families to take these songs and make them their own by singing and or playing along. This book contains all the lyrics and you can find the recordings on all streaming or download services.

Note for Grown Ups
Kids love adventure, but safety comes first! Please supervise young explorers, especially around water, crafting tools, and wild places. Feel free to modify any activity in this book to suit your family and local environment and conditions.

Happy little wild music making!
Claudia & Melissa

Contents

ANIMAL FAMILIES & ZOO CONSERVATION	1
BRAVE LIKE A LION & LION FACTS & FUN	5
CLOUDFOREST CHORUS & SOUNDSCAPE ECOLOGY	7
DONT BE SCARED OF BUGS (WE NEED BUGS)	11
EARTH KIND: WHAT CAN YOU DO?	15
ECHIDNA LULLABY & THE ECHIDNA ENIGMA	18
FEATHERS AND BONES (EXTINCTION ELEGY)	22
GIRAFFE SONG, FACTS & FUN	27
GO BABY RHINO GO & RHINO FACTS AND FUN	31
HAPPY LITTLE HONEYBEE	35
HIPPO HARMONY: THE RIVER HORSE	39
LOOPY THE INCHWORM	43
LOVE BIRDS LOVE	47
MUDDY PUDDLES (FROG SONG) & THE FROGS OF AOTEAROA	51
PANDA ON A PLANE	55
PEKAPEKA PUKAPUKA (NZ BAT)	59
PINK FLAMINGO FLING	63
RAINBOW WORLD (BIODIVERSITY)	67
ROLY POLY POLAR BEAR	71
TARA TUATARA (SURVIVORS OF THE DINOSAUR AGE)	75
THE LITTLE BLUE SUSHI SHOP PENGUINS	79
THE VERY BUSY SLOTH	83
THIS BOOK BELONGS TO EVERYONE (DNA)	87
WE ARE THE PLATYPUS	91
ZOO HULLABALOO: WHO CAN DANCE AT THE ZOO?	95
ABOUT THE CREATORS	99

LITTLE WILD ANIMALS SING FOR THE EARTH

ANIMAL FAMILIES

LYRICS

We got animal families in 2 by 2 and 3 by 3
There's zoo babies everywhere
Come on in and show you care

Our little tribe of kiwi's growing here at our city zoo
Recently the family's been expanding
Darling little featherlings
Stretching out on their first morning

Oh won't you come and see
Welcome to the family
Our little kiwi kinderling, longest beak and tiny wings
Join the tribe of kiwilings

Our flamingos are flamboyant here at our city zoo
Don't you know our family's been expanding
Fluffy gray flamingolings, cute as a button little things
Hanging out and having fun

Oh won't you come and see?
And welcome to the family
Our pink flamingo finery, a regiment of plumery
Rosy tinted colony

SCIENCE AND SONG

There is a romp of playful otter here at our city zoo
Recently our family's been expanding
So come and see the otterlings and welcome to the family
Little otters so divine, it's nearly swimming time

Ooo wee
Welcome to the family

All the zoos across the world
Are joining up to help preserve
The families and habitats of creatures big and small

And our spider monkey troop is growing
here at our city zoo
Recently the family's been expanding
Little spider monkeys, clinging on to dad and mummy
Flying high from tree to tree
It must be lovely

Ooo wee
Welcome to the family
Little spider monkey babes, curiouser everyday
Monkey business all the way

Stripy zebra dazzling, giraffes a towering
A lion's pride, a keeper's smile
Kea conspiracy, kororā chattering
Elephants a memory, red panda cuddling
Merry bound of wallaby, tiger cubs a tumbling
Tortoise Galapagos, so many families

Ooo wee
Welcome to the family
Ooo wee
Welcome to the family

(C) Claudia Robin Gunn, 2022

FIND OUT

ZOO CONSERVATION

Once upon a time, zoos were places where people came to point and stare at the rarities and oddities of the world, which were collected and housed in metal and concrete bunkers. The animals in such zoos often spent a grim and purposeless life far from their original homes. Today, many zoos are very different from the zoos of old, with a purpose of safeguarding animal families from going extinct.

Enclosures are enriched with elements of natural habitats to give zoo animals a life similar to what they would have had in the wild. Zookeepers work hard to provide variety for their animals. And most important of all, many zoos and wildlife centres are involved in conservation efforts, both by funding conservation in the wild, and by providing emergency care for wildlife. Some also breed birds and animals for release back into the wild. Human families can aid these conservation efforts too by supporting their local zoo or wildlife centre and learning more about these animals.

Sometimes, zoo populations have ended up being the last living examples of a species - and have provided the means for the wild to be repopulated. Some well-known examples include Przewalski's horse, Bermuda land snails, and the Arabian oryx. In an ideal world, animals would be protected in their own habitat. But zoos can provide a stopgap measure.

For example, in Aotearoa New Zealand, 9 out of 10 young kiwi in the wild die in their first six months of life, mostly killed by introduced mammals such as cats, dogs, rats and stoats. However, if raised in captivity until they are big enough to fend for themselves in the wild, over 6 out of 10 kiwi survive. That's a much better chance of survival!

The other part of making sure kiwi can survive in their native land is pest control - both removing pest species such as stoats and ferrets, and also keeping pet dogs under control in areas where kiwi live.

Investigation activity: Do you have a zoo near you? Find out if it is involved in any conservation activities. Can you get involved?

Diorama activity: make a habitat-in-a-box for your favourite animal. Research what its needs are - consider what it eats, where it sleeps, what sort of vegetation it spends time in, and what kind of enrichment activities it might need. Don't put a real animal in your box though - you could make a model instead.

SING FOR THE EARTH - LITTLE WILD ANIMALS

BRAVE LIKE A LION

Brave like a lion, brave like a lion
Do you wanna play like a lion?

I'm wearing my lion suit for book character day
I'm going as the lion in the meadow,
Daddy made the costume just yesterday
He stitched the ears, he made the tail
It's fluffy
Like a lion's tale should be
And I'm proud like a lion walking up to school
For book character day

And I'm gonna
Play like a lion, run like a lion
Be brave like a lion can be
And I'm gonna
Roar like a lion, be strong like a lion
Do you wanna play lions with me?

Other kids have a costume from the store
Some of them think mine's funny
But mine was made with love
So I don't mind if it's a little crinkly
Did you know mama lions do the hunting
Daddy lions do the big roar
Lion cubs do the tumbling
Let's play like a lion some more

We can
Play like a lion, run like a lion
Be brave like lions can be
We can
Roar like a lion be strong like a lion
Be brave like a lion with me

When I get home I ain't taking it off
I'm gonna be a lion cub again tomorrow
Cos I had fun like a lion, playing like a lion
Like the lion in the meadow

Now I'm gonna
Sleep like a lion, snuggle like a lion
Dream like a lion dream
And when I wake up I'm gonna stretch like a lion
Will you be a lion with me?

Play like a lion, brave like a lion
Daddy you're my favourite lion

(C) Claudia Robin Gunn, 2022

SING FOR THE EARTH - LITTLE WILD ANIMALS

FIND OUT

LION FACTS AND FUN

Lions have been symbols of brave guardianship or kingship since ancient times, appearing in the 'cradle of humanity' (ancient Mesopotamia, an area in the Middle East where some of the first civilisations appeared) around 7000 years ago!

In Babylon, they were associated with kings and appear in tiled mosaics found by archaeologists. Statues of lions guarding important places became popular in China at least 2000 years ago. And in medieval times, knights renowned for bravery were often given the nickname 'Lion', like the British king, Richard the Lionheart. Lions are often used in heraldry - that is, as symbols for a family or individual.

So, what makes lions brave? Well, it's mostly that they are at the top of the food chain. Nothing hunts lions apart from people. That probably appealed to ancient kings and knights!

Lions don't start off brave though - as cubs, they rely on their mother to defend them. Mother lions usually take their cubs away from the rest of the pride until they're big enough to cope with other lions. As adults, they spend up to twenty hours a day resting, rather than being brave!

Lions used to be more widespread. As well as living in Africa and India, lions used to roam southern Europe. In the last ice age, there were also Eurasian and North American cave lions.

ACTIVITY

Craft Activity: Make yourself a lion shield or tunic. Lions are often drawn rising up on their hind legs ('rampant'), but you can draw a lion any way you like. They do like to sleep after all!

Sketch your ideas on paper first, then use cardboard for a shield, or if you're lucky enough to have a t-shirt you can paint, use that for a tunic. Paint your final design onto your shield or tunic, then step out bravely.

SCIENCE AND SONG

CLOUD FOREST CHORUS

LYRICS

In the cloud forest canopy the songbirds call
All the hummingbirds and toucans and
Umbrella birds and more
If you walk down below among the orchid blooms
Don't forget to look up and see the colours up there too

Hear the cloud forest chorus
The cloud forest song
Hear the hummingbirds and toucans
And umbrella birds and more

In the cloud forest you might see the spectacled bear
Yellow tailed woolly monkey or the mountain tapir
If you walk down below be sure to look around
In the cloud forest magic may always be raining down

Hear the cloud forest chorus
It's a cloud forest song
Hear the hummingbirds and toucans
And umbrella birds and more
It's a cloud forest chorus of biodiversity
If we wanna hear the chorus
We must save the trees

There are many kinds of wildlife in the cloudforest shade
Like the rain frog, tortoise beetle and the giant snail

It's a cloud forest chorus, a cloud forest song
Let the hummingbirds and toucans
And umbrella birds live long
It's a cloud forest chorus of biodiversity
If we wanna hear the chorus
We must save the trees

(C) Claudia Robin Gunn, 2022

FIND OUT

SOUNDSCAPE ECOLOGY

Have you ever woken up early and listened to the chatter and chirp of the dawn chorus? Maybe you've wondered how on earth the birds can hear each other in the din! Well, it turns out that scientists have wondered the same thing. Since the 1970s, scientists have been studying the range of sounds (the 'soundscape') made by animals and their environment. This is sometimes called soundscape ecology.

It is becoming easier than ever to study the sounds around us, because batteries and remote data retrieval (microphones that send their information to someone on the internet) mean that scientists don't have to be on the spot to hear what's going on. Someone in Aotearoa New Zealand could listen to sounds in tropical jungles, pretty much as they happen!

Some scientists believe that animals evolve to fill every part of a soundscape – so some animals will use high sounds (like pekapeka/bats), some animals will use not-quite-so-high sounds (like tauhou/silvereyes), some will use low sounds (like kōkako singing in the mist, or kākāpō booming in their leks), and other animals, birds or insects will fill in the middle (like tui). If an animal goes extinct in an area, then there will be a gap in the soundscape.

It's a different problem underwater, and in busy traffic areas. There, human-made sound can overwhelm natural sounds. For example, motorboats cause a lot of sound pollution underwater, making it difficult for animals like dolphins and whales to use their sonar (where they make clicks or other noises to find food or locate objects like boats). In noisy areas, like beside motorways, birds will sing less complicated songs, because their more intricate songs can't be heard.

Listening Activity: Listen to your favourite soundscape! Go on an expedition to your backyard, or to the beach, or perhaps the bush. You can even do this lying in bed at night. Then listen carefully - what different sounds can you hear? Try listening for sounds that are deeper, sounds that are higher, and sounds that are in the middle. Is one section of sound louder than the others? Can you identify all the sounds you hear? You might find some sounds dominate the rest - are they human-made sounds or natural ones? This is an activity you can do again and again. Try it at different times of day and in different places to see what variety of sounds you hear.

Advanced listening activity: Record what you hear (for example with a smartphone or other recording device) and look at the soundwaves using audio software like Audacity. You might be able to pick out the different parts of the soundscape as you play it back. Are there any quiet spots in your soundscape?

DON'T BE SCARED OF BUGS

I'm a busy honeybee, I'm a daring dragonfly
I'm an Archeys frog, I'm a katipō hiding in the driftwood
I'm a happy huhu grub, I'm a little blue ladybug
I'm a red admiral butterfly (Don't be scared of bugs)

Insects, amphibians,
arachnids and invertebrates
Bugs are many; bugs are very
interesting and numerous
Don't be scared of bugs

I'm a silky spinning spider, I'm a shy and secret slater
I'm a pink and wriggly earthworm, keeping all the soil turned
I'm a copper caterpillar, I'm a giant wētāpunga
I'm a powelliphanta snail (Don't be scared of bugs)

SCIENCE AND SONG

Insects, amphibians,
arachnids and invertebrates
Bugs are many; bugs are varied,
interesting and numerous
Insects, amphibians,
arachnids and invertebrates
Bugs are many; bugs are very
interesting and numerous

Don't be scared of bugs
Don't call us names or make a nasty fuss
We're just little bugs in a big big world
Come on now

Insects, amphibians,
arachnids and invertebrates
Bugs are many; bugs are very
interesting and numerous
Insects, amphibians,
arachnids and invertebrates
We are many, we are varied,
interesting and numerous
Don't be scared of bugs

I'm a three eyed tuatara, I'm a stick insect in the mānuka
I'm a bright green beautiful puriri moth
flying aloft for just one night

I'm a glow worm shining by the river
(don't be scared of bugs)
I'm a cicada in the summer (don't be scared of bugs)
I'm a giant centipede (don't be scared of bugs)
Hiding in the leaves

Da da da (Don't be scared of bugs)
Da da da (Don't be scared of bugs)
Da da da da da da da
Da da da da da (Just a little bug!)
Don't be scared of bugs

(C) Claudia Robin Gunn, 2022

WE NEED BUGS

Creepy, crawly, icky, bugs... or fascinating, intriguing, essential bugs? How do you feel about bugs? Love them or loathe them, they're all around us. And it turns out, we need them! They're an essential part of the ecosystem.

Let's start with some of our most disliked bugs. A lot of people hate mosquitos, but they're an important part of the diet of pīwakawaka (fantail). In fact, many small birds wouldn't survive without flying, biting insects.

What about cockroaches? They scuttle into our houses and surprise us with their night-time emergence. But they're just looking out for decaying vegetation. Without the army of bugs that feed on old leaves, the world would be piled high with dead plants.

Worms are slippery, slimy friends, inching their way across footpaths on rainy mornings, but usually hidden underground, turning leaves into soil. Without them, we wouldn't have much to garden.

Everyone hates an ant invasion in the kitchen. But without ants, the garbage renewal crews of the world, we'd be living in a world full of rubbish. Ants take care of everything from rotting vegetables to dead insects.

Even wasps, perhaps the most hated insect of all (at least when they crash our picnics with their yellow-striped armour and scary stings) have an important role in their native range, eating other insects and pollinating flowers.

Then of course there is everyone's favourite bug, the bee. Bees are responsible for pollinating around a third of the world's food crops. We wouldn't have much to eat without them. There are native bees, too, which pollinate some of New Zealand's favourite flowers, from pōhutukawa to mānuka.

Citizen Science Activity: When you're out walking in nature, look out for patches of bare earth on banks or dry patches of ground, with little holes in them (about 1-2mm wide). In springtime and summer, some of the holes will have tiny mounds of dust next to them. Those are the holes which are nests for solitary native bees. You can measure an area including nests (about 30cm by 30cm is good) and count the number of active nests.

In spring or early summer, watch for a while and see if you can spot any bees coming and going. Then look around. Each colony of native bees tends to be associated with a particular tree or group of trees. Look for flowering pōhutukawa, hebe or mānuka. If you're lucky, you might find the bee tree of your native bee colony! Check out this resource to find out more about NZ native bees:

https://www.fortheloveofbees.co.nz/native-bees

Each country has their own native bees. Find out about yours!

SING FOR THE EARTH - LITTLE WILD ANIMALS

EARTH KIND

If I had 100 hearts
I would give em all away
To make the world a kinder place
Even better than it is today
If I had 100 dollar bills
I would make a great big cake
Made of every kind of food my friends would like
And share it with all earthkind

For we all have countless gifts that we can give
And we can make a difference
even if we're still just little kids
For we all have limitless love and courage and hope
When we find it, hold strong, for this is how we roll

Count it up for all earthkind
You know the count goes on and on
Count it up we're counting on
Infinity goes on and on

SCIENCE AND SONG

If I had 100 stars in my hands
I would throw them right back to the sky
I'd never let the Milky Way go dark
We should all share the light
If I had 100 years
I would try to make the most of
Every single second
Cos no one knows just how much they're given

For we all have countless gifts that we can give
And we can make a difference
even if we're still kids
For we all have boundless love and courage and hope
When we find it, hold strong, for this is how we roll

Count it up for all earthkind
You know the count goes on and on
Count it up we're counting on
Infinity goes on
Count it up for all earthkind
And the count goes on and on
Count it up we're counting on
Infinity goes on and on and on and on and on
Be kind, for all earthkind

(C) Claudia Robin Gunn, 2022

WHAT CAN YOU DO?
(TO BE EARTH KIND)

For 50 years or more, people around the world have been celebrating Earth Day. It's an opportunity to raise awareness and take action on issues around conservation and climate change. Perhaps this year you can celebrate Earth Day too. It's held on the 22nd April, and there are usually a range of events organised around the world.

But you don't have to wait for Earth Day to swing around to seek out ways to be kind to our planet - every day is a day to find out what you can do to help reduce the effects of climate change, or improve local habitat for wildlife.

While biodiversity loss and climate change can seem like big problems, lots of small helpful actions can really add up.

Activity: Kids really can make a difference. Plant a tree, build a lizard lounge, count birds or animals. Pick up rubbish to reduce litter going to the sea or being eaten by animals. Reuse what you can, recycle what you can't. Eat less meat. There's lots of ways we can be kind to the Earth every day, for the sake of all earthkind; humans, animals, plants alike.

ECHIDNA LULLABY

I am little spiky but I promise I'm not scary
I only have these spines to keep me safe
Inside I'm just a softie
I am a little baby, a lil' Echidna baby
So please don't be afraid, I love to play
Oh won't you play a game?

We could roll roll roll roll roll roll roll away
We could roll roll roll roll roll roll roll away

If I'm a little prickly, its only cos I'm hiding
When I roll into a ball or dig a hole
It's cos I need to hide away
I am a little baby, a lil' Echidna baby
Oh please don't be afraid, I love to play
Oh won't you play a game?

We could dig dig dig dig dig dig underground
Can you dig dig dig dig dig dig just like me?
We can roll roll roll roll roll roll roll away
We can roll roll roll roll roll roll roll away
(roll roll roll roll roll roll roll)
We could roll roll roll roll roll roll roll away
(roll roll roll roll roll roll roll)
We could roll roll roll roll roll roll roll away
(roll roll roll roll roll roll roll)
We could roll roll roll roll roll roll roll away
(roll roll roll roll roll roll roll away)
We could roll roll roll roll roll roll roll away

We are a little spiky, but we're not scary
We only have these spines to keep us safe

Can you roll roll roll roll roll roll away?
Can you dig dig dig dig underground?
Can you roll roll roll roll roll roll away?
Roll away, roll away

(C) Claudia Robin Gunn, 2022

ECHIDNA ENIGMA

Like their Australian cousin, the platypus, the echidna is an egg-laying mammal, or monotreme. There are echidna living wild in just two countries, Australia and New Guinea.

The echidna has the second-lowest body temperature for a mammal – just a bit warmer than the platypus. Unlike the platypus, it looks a bit like an overgrown hedgehog, because it is covered with spiny quills! Like other spiny mammals, the spines are formed of keratin, the same thing that makes fingernails and hair. Their spines protect them from predation. They can curl up into an impenetrable ball of spikes when disturbed, but baby echidna (known as puggles) don't have spines, so they are especially vulnerable to predators such as snakes which can enter their nursery burrows.

Echidna are sometimes called spiny anteaters, because they eat ants, termites and worms, which they find using electrosensors on their beaks (just like the platypus, except on dry land). They have less electrosensors than platypus, and are said to detect vibrations with their beaks, too.

Mating is very competitive in echidnas, and males will form an echidna 'train' behind females when attempting to mate, with the youngest male last in the train. Interestingly, echidna lay one egg from their cloaca (like birds), which they transfer into a temporary pouch formed by strong muscles on their abdomen (the outside

of their tummy). Both males and females can form this pouch, but only females look after the egg, which is held there for several days before the puggle hatches. The puggle stays in the mother's pouch until it begins to grow quills (ouch!). It laps milk from milk-patches; like the platypus, echidna have no external nipples.

There are four species of echidna, which are divided into two types: long-beaked and short-beaked. The three long-beaked echidna are found in New Guinea, while the short-beaked species is found in a huge range of habitats all over Australia. The short-beaked echidna look very different depending on where they are in Australia, so they're sorted into more sub-species.

Echidna will often use rock crevices, wombat or rabbit burrows to shelter from extreme temperatures, including bushfires. They are also surprisingly good swimmers, and have been known to walk some distance to go bathing. Echidna also hibernate to get through winter. Curiously, they can only experience REM sleep (that part of sleep when we dream) when the temperature is below 25 degrees C. That suggests they can only dream when it's cool!

Activity: Make a den or fort suitable for an echidna to dream in! That means it should be dark, comfortable and cool. Try using blankets or sheets and some chairs as a basis for your fort.

SCIENCE AND SONG

FEATHERS & BONES
EXTINCTION ELEGY

LYRICS

I have been raised by the river
I have been raised in the trees
I have been raised in the mountains and plains
Just like the creatures that came before me

Eagles flew here before us
Eagles flew years ago
Eagles flew here but now they're long gone
This is the Haast eagle's song

Moa walked here by the river
Moa walked here years ago
Moa walked here but now they're long gone
This is the great moa's song

Huia sung here before us
Huia sung years ago
Huia sung here but now they're long gone
So this is a tribute song

SING FOR THE EARTH - LITTLE WILD ANIMALS

Grayling swum here before us
Grayling swum years ago
Grayling swum here but now they're long gone
This is those grayling's song

I have been raised by the river
I have been raised in the trees
I have been raised in the mountains and plains
Just like the creatures that came before me

And I will remember the eagle
And I will rejoice in its flight
Though I never saw it or heard the wingbeats
The Haast eagle soars through the night

And I will remember the moa
And I will respect the great bones
Though I wasn't here nor my mothers before me
This was the great moa's home

And I will remember the huia
And I will imagine their song
Those white tipped feathers and legendary voices
This is the place they belonged

I will remember the grayling
I will recall they swum up from the sea
Then forests fell and choked up the rivers
Now graylings are history

I have been raised by the river
I have been raised in the trees
I have been raised in the mountains and plains
Just like the creatures that came before me
And they can be found in the rivers
They can be found in the trees
They can be found in the mountains and plans
The bones and the fossils and feathers of creatures
That came before me

(C) Claudia Robin Gunn, 2022

SCIENCE AND SONG

EXTINCTIONS IN AOTEAROA

Extinction is what we call it when there are no more living animals of a particular type. One of the most famous extinctions is that of the dinosaurs. But there are many more recent extinctions, too recent for there to be fossils. All that's left of these recently extinct species are feathers and bones.

New Zealand has an unfortunate history of recent extinctions, including fish, birds, plants and insects. Some of these animals we know from stories, like the mighty pouakai bird, or the hōkioi, which people think were Haast's eagles, the mightiest eagle ever to fly, with a wingspan over 3 metres wide.

We know of other extinct animals from their feathers and bones – like the moa, which Haast's eagle depended on for food. There were nine species of moa, all flightless, ranging from quite small to up to four metres tall. Both moa and eagle died out around 500 years ago, probably from a combination of habitat destruction and hunting.

The huia is NZ's most well-known extinction. A unique and beautiful bird, the huia was considered tapu (sacred). Males and females had different-shaped beaks, enabling them to access insects in different parts of rotting wood. They depended on old-growth forest, both as a source of food and because they were pretty bad at flying and needed lots of branches to hop around on.

But old-growth forest was chopped down; stoats, cats and rats were introduced, and huia were hunted for their prized black and white tailfeathers. All this meant the last confirmed sighting of huia was way back in 1907. Less well-known is the extinction of the huia louse which depended on the huia for survival! As the huia were no longer around, the huia louse died out too.

There are knock-on effects of extinction for the whole ecosystem; moa had a key role in shaping New Zealand plant life. Huia, and other fruit-eating birds like the also-extinct piopio, were essential for spreading seeds for many NZ trees.

The world is a poorer place without these birds (and louse). Habitat destruction is a common theme in these extinctions. And it's not a thing of the past; in Aotearoa New Zealand and around the world, habitat is being destroyed or degraded faster than ever. Nearly three quarters of New Zealand bird species are at risk of extinction. Nine out of ten of our reptiles are too.

Activity: It's up to us to make sure our remaining wildlife doesn't go the way of the huia, the huia louse, the moa and Haast's eagle.

Action 1. Take action in your own backyard or local environment and provide some habitat for lizards by making a lizard lounge! You will need a dry, sunny spot in your garden, preferably with some native plants nearby. Next, you need some found materials - old pieces of wood, sheets of corrugated iron, stones. Pile them up, leaving cracks and crevices for lizards to hide in - this gives them safe spots to bask in the sun, with hidey-holes nearby so they can escape predators.

Action 2. Find out if there is a local predator-free group in your area. Can you join it? Backyard pest removal can help. You can also help by keeping pet dogs on a leash when you're out in nature. Tell people about the wonderful world you see around you.

SING FOR THE EARTH - LITTLE WILD ANIMALS

GIRAFFE SONG

Ooooh
Sometimes I wish I could be a giraffe
Head stretched up high in the leaves
I would pretend a giraffe's what I am
And my friends had long necks like me

Heads high up in the sky
Imagine how much we could see
We'd sleep standing up
Clean our ears with our tongues
Oh what a life that would be

Ooooooh
Sometimes I'd love to be a giraffe
Head stretched high in the leaves
My friends and I so tall together
Singing giraffe songs like these
Heads high up in the sky
All of the world we can see

We'd sleep standing up
Clean our ears with our tongues
See our spot patterns; unique every one
Munch on acacia leaves
No lions thank you team
This is the life for me
Ooooooh

Sometimes I need to be a giraffe
Head stretched high in the leaves
My friends and I so tall together
Swaying with the beautiful breeze

SCIENCE AND SONG

Heads high up in the sky
All of the world we can see
We'd sleep standing up
Clean our ears with our tongues
See our spot patterns: unique every one
Munch on acacia leaves
No lions thank you team
When we drink water we drop to our
knees This is the long legged long necked
Longest drink in town
Long seeing life for me

    Oooooh
    Oooooh
    Oooooh
    Oooooh

(C) Claudia Robin Gunn, 2022

GIRAFFE FACTS AND FUN

The giraffe is well-known as an African mammal with long legs and a longer neck. But did you know that there were once giraffes in southern Europe and Asia? Over millennia, they moved into Africa, where they evolved into the animals we know and love today. The Asian and European versions are long extinct. But in Africa (and in zoos around the world) there are still eight or so species of giraffe. The exact species divisions change from time to time as scientists find evidence for similarities and differences.

While all giraffes have long legs and necks, and are spotted (the old English name for giraffe was camelopardis, meaning leopard-coloured camel), the size and colour of the spots varies a lot. Some have more white around the coloured spots; some have darker coloured spots. It's important for zoos and scientists to understand which species is which, so that breeding programs to help conserve giraffes don't mix them up.

Every individual giraffe has a different spot pattern, which can be used to tell them apart. Some people think that the spots help them camouflage. But since giraffes are really, really big, other people consider that camouflage is only important for calves, which are much more vulnerable to predators.

People used to think that giraffes were silent. But it turns out that they actually hum to each other at night! They use infrasound, which people don't hear so well because it is such a low sound. They can also hiss, snort, and grunt. Male giraffes sometimes battle using a technique called 'necking', where they try to hit each other's necks. Afterwards, they make up, grooming one another.

In the wild, giraffes live in groups of different sizes. When zebra and giraffe are browsing in the same area, zebra pay attention to giraffe behaviour to alert them to predators. Like many animals, giraffe are under threat from habitat loss. They're also at risk from hunting for bushmeat. So long as trees are left in place, giraffe can co-exist with farm animals, since they eat leaves high up, rather than grass low down.

Because of their very long necks, giraffe have some unusual adaptations. Their hearts are really big (weighing about 11 kilograms!), and they have very tight skin on their legs to keep blood from pooling in their legs (which could make them faint). When they need to drink, they often spread their front legs apart so as to reach water at ground level. And they have a blue-black tongue, which they can use to pluck leaves from amongst spiny branches. Some people think the colour stops it from getting sunburnt!

Activity: Make a sock puppet giraffe. Find a long, worn-out sock, paint it to your liking, cut out and glue on eyes, nostrils and horns and ears made out of paper. Do this activity with a friend and you could put on a mini giraffe puppet show complete with this song, or play a game together to see how many leaves you can pick with your sock puppet.

GO BABY RHINO GO

Go baby rhino go, run baby rhino run
Stop baby rhino stop, and then we'll start all over again
Go baby rhino go, run baby rhino run
Stop baby rhino stop, and then we'll start all over again

Rhino baby rhino I can play you on a jukebox
Any song you wanna listen to
As long as it sounds like do ba de dop do ba de dop
Run baby rhino run and stop

Rhino baby rhino I can see you're growing stronger
And faster everyday
Don't let anybody slow you down
or tell ya to take it easy

Go baby rhino go
Stop baby rhino stop
And when the day is done and we've had all our fun

Sleep baby rhino sleep, dream baby rhino dream
Soon baby rhino soon, you'll wake up and start over again

Go baby rhino go, run baby rhino run
Stop baby rhino stop, and then we'll start all over again
Go baby rhino go, oh run baby rhino run
Stop baby rhino stop, and then we'll start all over again
And then we'll start all over again
Start all over again

Now rest baby rhino rest, snooze baby rhino snooze
Dream baby rhino dream, then we'll start all over again

(C) Claudia Robin Gunn, 2022

FIND OUT: RHINO FACTS AND FUN

Rhinoceros, often known as rhinos, are one of the world's biggest remaining megafauna (literally, big animals). They have thick, armour-like skin, and very little hair. Instead of front teeth, they use their lips to pluck grass or leaves.

Rhino babies can walk within an hour of being born. After a few days, they can run, up to 50km per hour! It's quite something to see such a big animal barrelling along.

There are 5 different species of rhino still alive today. The biggest of them can weigh more than 2 and a 1/2 tons. Males are usually larger than females. Sadly, most species of rhino are either endangered or vulnerable. The African white and black rhino are probably the most well-known species. Despite what you might think from the name, neither of these rhinoceros' hides are black or white. In fact, they are both shades of grey. There are also subspecies within those species. One subspecies, the northern white rhino, consists of only 2 female animals; it is pretty much extinct. Other rhino species are in trouble too. There are Indian rhinos, Sumatran rhinos, and rarest of all, the Javan rhino.

Why are they so rare? It depends on the species. Rhino are often hunted for their horns. The one, two, or even three horns that grow on their noses are made of the same thing as our hair and fingernails: keratin. For some reason, people value rhino horns more than fingernail trimmings, and are prepared to kill rhinos to get them.

The world's rarest species of rhino, the Javan rhino, faces a number of threats, not just the threat of poachers. The hairiest of the rhinos (and a relative of the woolly rhino of ice age times) Javan rhino prefer thick forest. That forest is being logged and transformed into palm oil plantations. Invasive weeds that take over the rhino's preferred foods are also a problem.

There's one funny thing that African rhino do. They make dung middens. That means they all poop in the same spot. When adding to the pile, they sniff it, apparently getting a wealth of information from doing so!

Activity: Support tropical rainforest protection and help save rhino habitat in the wild by choosing to refuse to buy food or grocery items that include palm oil products or their derivatives. You'll need to have a conversation with grown-ups about why you want to do this. Some palm oil is okay - that's when it's grown in a sustainable way, without deforestation. Find out more about palm oil here: https://www.aucklandzoo.co.nz/get-involved/palm-oil

Maths activity: Find out how much space two and a half tonnes would take up if was all water! Here's some clues to help you out: 1 tonne is 1000 kilograms. 1 litre of water weighs 1 kilogram. Now all you have to do is do some multiplication!

Hint: find 1 litre container (like a small empty milk bottle) and count how many of those you'd need to get to 2.5 x 1000, to help you imagine how big a rhino can really be.

SING FOR THE EARTH - LITTLE WILD ANIMALS

HAPPY LITTLE HONEYBEE

Buzz buzz, buzz buzz

You're my happy little honeybee
You're my happy little honeybee
You get smiles from all the fruit trees
You spread the love - to everyone you meet
Buzz buzz buzz buzz

You're my happy little honeybee
You got pollen on your dusty feet
You bring life to all the flowers
Cos you spread the love everywhere you been
Buzz buzz buzz buzz
Oh happy little honeybee
Oh happy little honeybee

I see you buzz buzz buzzing round and round
I see you pollinating flowers all around the town
Show me how you dance wiggle left and wiggle right
When ya tell your friends the way to find the flowers
Blooming bright
Buzz buzz buzz buzz
Buzz buzz buzz buzz

Thank you happy little honeybee
Thank you happy little honey bee
You bring smiles to all the garden
And all the flowers and all the trees
You spread the love everywhere you've been

(C) Claudia Robin Gunn, 2022

SCIENCE AND SONG

HONEYBEES EVERYWHERE

Honeybees are found almost everywhere that people live. Humans like honey so much, we have taken bees with us – from Africa and Europe to the Americas, Australia, and New Zealand. Antarctica is possibly the one exception. Bees have even been sent into space! They didn't like it much though – not enough flowers, or gravity.

Of course, bees do more than make honey. Honeybees also pollinate crops. Some people think that bees are responsible for pollinating up to a third of our food crops. That means we really do depend on our honeybee friends.

Honey bees are most common in summer, because the honeybee queen lays thousands of eggs a day in spring. Most of those eggs hatch into female worker bees, who spend their summer gathering nectar and pollen from flowers, building and filling honeycomb, tending the eggs which hatch into larvae, feeding and tending the queen, feeding the males (drones) and generally buzzing busily around! Luckily they don't fly at night, or they wouldn't rest at all.

Honeybees are world-class communicators, using peeps, buzzing, stylized dancing and scent to convey information in their hives. They are social insects, which means they work for the good of the hive, more than the good of any individual bee – teamwork taken to extremes!

Apis mellifera (European honeybee) hives can hold up to 60,000 bees in the height of summer, all working together to store honey for winter. Each teaspoon of honey takes a lifetime's work for 12 bees (where a lifetime is about 6 weeks - typical for summer bees).

Bees see a different colour range to humans, which means that flowers look different to them. What look like plain white flowers to humans could actually have glowing patches which direct the bee towards the flower's nectar. Some flowers even make their nectar sweeter when they detect a bee buzzing nearby. Unfortunately, some pesticides also smell sweet to bees, with bad results for bee memory and survival.

Honeybees will fly in and out of their hive following their own flight paths. If you get a chance to see a bee-hive, watch for a while (from a distance!) and see if you can see some flight paths.

Honeybee Feeding Activity: make a bee water bowl. Fill a shallow bowl with marbles. Find a spot to put it, at least 50cm off the ground. Now fill it with water. Bees should be able to crawl on the marbles in order to drink the water, without falling in (bees aren't swimmers). Don't add honey, because it can pass on bee diseases.

Advanced activity: Talk to your family about avoiding sprays in your garden, and letting the weeds and flowers grow in your lawn instead to allow for a bee friendly backyard. You could even find a bee-keeping club and ask if they give talks!

HIPPO HARMONY

It's a 'ippo, 'ippo-onomus

CHORUS
Come and join our hippo harmony
Sing a little merry melody
Cos I know a little hippo
Who's hip hip hopping along

Hip hip hippo, dancing everywhere she goes
Hip hop hippo, bubbles when she blows
Hip hip hippo, hip hip hopping along

REPEAT CHORUS

Hippopotamus!

Tell me how you say it hip hip hippo
'Hippaponamus', happy hoppy hippo
'Hoppotopatus', happy hoppy hippo
Hip hip hopping along

It's a hippopotamus!

SCIENCE AND SONG

REPEAT CHORUS

Can you sing the bass part?
That's low down here
Can you sing the alto?
In the middle no problem
Can you sing soprano?
That's high – up high
Three part harmony
It's so easy

REPEAT CHORUS

Hippopotamus

Tell me how you say it hip hip hippo
Hoppiponamoss *(It's a hippo)* hip hop hippo
Hippapippamus happy hoppy hippo
Happiponomonomoss
Oh oh

It's a hippopotamus!

REPEAT CHORUS

Join our hippo harmony
Sing a little merry melody
Cos I know a little hippo
Who's hip hip hopping along
All together now

Come and join our hippo harmony
Sing a little merry melody
Cos I know a little hippo
Who's hip hip hopping along
Oh oh hip hip hopping along
Oh oh hip hip hopping along

Hippopotamus!

(C) Claudia Robin Gunn, 2022

THE RIVER HORSE

Hippopotamus, or 'river horse' are a well-known, well-rounded animal hailing from Africa. Although they more closely resemble pigs, their closest relatives are actually cetaceans - that is, whales & dolphins. Just like their aquatic relatives, hippos need to spend a large amount of time in water - most often freshwater lakes and rivers, but they are sometimes found in estuaries, or even out to sea!

They spend the day sleeping underwater, rising to the surface to breathe from time to time without even waking up. Unlike dolphins, they sleep with both sides of their brains, so when they're asleep, they're really asleep. Hippo calves are born underwater, and they can suckle their mother's milk while submerged.

As the day cools off, hippopotamuses will emerge to eat grass on land, where they can gallop at up to 30km per hour. Due to their size and aggression, not many animals dare to attack a full-grown hippo. Only hippopotamus calves are at risk from carnivores.

Hippo are the most dangerous land mammal, due to their unpredictable nature, and ability to move fast both on land and in the water. Bull (male) hippos are also territorial (but only in the water), protecting the stretch of water where their pod of females live. Bull hippos will yawn as a threat, displaying their large teeth.

Not all hippopotamus are large. There is a pygmy hippo which lives in West Africa, and there used to be several dwarf hippos on islands such as Madagascar, Crete and Cyprus.

Hippopotamus take good care of their thick skin; they naturally secrete a red-coloured sunscreen to help protect them from the sun. They will also occasionally visit cleaning stations, where fish remove their parasites.

Activity: Hippo Bath Time (parent supervision required!) Play some hippopotamus songs, blow some bubbles, and you could even apply your own hippo mud mask made of oatmeal!

Ask your parents to help you make this kid-safe hippo face mask for your skin: Method: Mix 2 TBSP lukewarm water with ¼ cup finely ground oatmeal (you can use millet or quinoa if you are allergic to oats) and let this sit for 10 minutes. Add 1 TBSP plain yogurt to the mix and stir. You can also add 1 TSP of honey for softness (so long as you are not allergic). Apply gently to your forehead, cheeks and nose, and let it dry while you have your bath then wash it off just like a hippo would do!

SING FOR THE EARTH – LITTLE WILD ANIMALS

LYRICS

LOOPY THE INCHWORM

I found a little inchworm
Inching up an oak tree
Looping in a funny way
Doubled up and back again
It crawled onto a leaf and up my arm
It must have thought that I was a little acorn

And I got a kind of loopy love
Got me doing inchworm stuff
Like this bendy stretchy yoga pose
Now I can touch my knees with my nose

Now Loopy goes where I go,
inching up my headphones
Looping in a funny way
Doubled up and back again
After looping all day it's time to sleep
And Loopy snuggles up on an oak leaf

SCIENCE AND SONG

Now I got a kind of loopy love
It's got me doing inchworm stuff
Like this bendy stretchy yoga pose
Now I can touch my knees with my nose

I love Loopy, Loopy loves me
I love Loopy, Loopy loves me

Goodbye my little inchworm,
looping up your oak tree
Looping in your funny way,
doubled up and back again
Inchworm, inchworm, inchworm

I got a kind of loopy love
It's got me doing inchworm stuff
Like this bendy stretchy yoga pose
Now I can touch my knees with my nose

I just got a kind of loopy love
It's got me doing inchworm stuff
Like this bendy stretchy yoga pose
Now I can touch my knees with my nose

I love Loopy, Loopy loves me
I love Loopy, Loopy loves me

(C) Claudia Robin Gunn, 2022

SING FOR THE EARTH - LITTLE WILD ANIMALS

FIND OUT

MOVE LIKE LOOPY

Have you ever seen an inchworm or a looper caterpillar moving about?

They have a very special way of moving their bodies, hunching their backs high in the air before raising their whole body to reach for the next place on a leaf. They have to move this way because they have legs at the front of their bodies and claspers (another sort of leg) at the end, but no legs in between. Some people call these caterpillars 'measuring worms', because with each move they measure out the same distance (they're not really worms, mind you).

Inchworm is the common name for a large group of caterpillars including lots of different species - over 35,000! They usually turn into moths of different types. For example, a common 'inchworm' is the garden looper caterpillar, which is bright green. Aotearoa New Zealand has lots of different looper caterpillars, like the kawakawa looper moth which causes all the holes in healthy kawakawa leaves.

Activity: Be an inchworm with yoga moves! Start off stretching high, like an inchworm reaching for the sky. Lean down towards your toes, leaving your back(side) high in the air. This is your looper caterpillar moment! Now walk your hands forward till you're forming a triangle with the ground (this is a move called downward dog). Keep going until your arms are supporting your body and you are perpendicular to the ground, feet on tippy toes. Now walk your feet forward to join your hands again. And repeat! You can be an inchworm too.

When you're done inching your way around, roll yourself slowly up to stand on your feet again and give yourself a hug.

SING FOR THE EARTH - LITTLE WILD ANIMALS

LOVEBIRDS LOVE

Lovebirds love
Lovebirds love
Lovebirds love
(oooh)

Lovebirds love to sing for you and I
And always stay together
Lovebirds love to share their joy
With you and I, true love forever

Lovebirds love to love to give
Lovebirds love to love to wish
Their lovely thoughts into the world
To all the lovely hearts and souls

SCIENCE AND SONG

Lovebirds love to dance in twos
In lovely ballroom tippy toe dance moves
Lovebirds love to share their joy
With you and I, true love forever

Lovebirds love to love to shine
Their lovely lovely love bird style
And this I know, I know is true
That lovebirds love birds always do

Love to love to sing
Love to love to dance
Love to love to give
Love to love to take a chance

Lovebirds love to sing and share
And dance and give and shine and wish
Lovebirds love to stay together
Lovebirds love true love forever

(oooh)
Lovebirds love
(oooh)
Lovebirds love
(oooh)
Lovebirds love

(C) Claudia Robin Gunn, 2022

SNUGGLY LOVE BIRDS

Have you ever watched a pair of lovebirds snuggling up to each other? If so, you already know how they got their name! Lovebirds are extremely affectionate with their mates, cuddling close and preening one another. That's good a thing, since they mate for life, all going well (up to 15 years). Bonded lovebirds will feed each other after times of separation or stress. But don't be fooled, it's not all lovey-dovey - they can be mean or jealous of other birds, especially non-lovebirds. They naturally live in large flocks which are quite territorial - that's why lovebirds in zoos usually have a large aviary all to themselves.

Lovebirds are African parrots who love to talk to each other. They're not keen on learning human language though, being quite content with their own. There are nine species of lovebirds, all native to Africa or Madagascar. While some species are quite common, others are 'vulnerable' (black-faced lovebirds) or 'near-threatened'. The main difficulty facing wild lovebirds is loss of habitat. They typically live in forests and savannas, so when these are logged or built on, their living space and food source disappears.

Lovebirds are herbivores, eating fruit, seeds, or vegetation (depending on the species). They make their nests in holes. Masked lovebirds like to make a false nest, with a tunnel underneath it leading to the real nest, where the eggs are laid and the female incubates them. The male of the pair makes sure his partner and their chicks are fed until the chicks fledge, about a month after hatching.

Lovebirds also have a secret superpower: they can turn their heads superfast during flight (about 270 degrees per second - remember, 360 degrees is a full circle, so they can really whip their heads around quickly). That's faster than a human can blink! This helps them avoid collisions when flying in dense flocks in cluttered environments like forests.

Activity: Be a friend and write a kind note to someone. It doesn't have to be Valentine's day to show someone you care. It might just make their day.

SING FOR THE EARTH - LITTLE WILD ANIMALS

I jumped in a puddle right up to my middle
It was muddy, it was deep and it was cold!
It got me in a muddle; it was actually a pond
A little frog jumped out and said won't you sing along?

Muddy puddles are the best (he sang)
But sometimes puddles turn into ponds
Muddy puddles are a frog's best friend
I hope you're gonna stay and jump with me til the end
Ribbet

I said I only wanted a tiny little splash
The kind that gets your trousers wet
And dries off in a flash
The froggy said "Well now you're here
You might as well jump in
We can have sploshy splashy muddly puddly swim"

SCIENCE AND SONG

Muddy puddles are the best (he sang)
But sometimes puddles turn into ponds
Muddy puddles are a frog's best friend
I hope you're gonna stay and jump with me til the end
Ribbet

I splosh in my galoshes, the water's everywhere
My pants are dripping and the drops are even in my hair
The rain is coming down in waves, better race inside
I wave goodbye to Mr Frog and in the pond he dives

Muddy puddles are the best (he sang)
Sometimes puddles turn into ponds
Muddy puddles are a frog's best friend
I hope you're gonna jump on by and visit again
Muddy puddles are the best (I sang)
Sometimes puddles turn into ponds
Muddy puddles are a frog's best friend
I know I'm gonna jump on into this puddle again

(C) Claudia Robin Gunn, 2022

SING FOR THE EARTH - LITTLE WILD ANIMALS

ANCIENT FROGS OF AOTEAROA

Everyone knows about frogs, right? They're green, they start off as tadpoles, they croak a lot, they hang around in ponds...

Well, stop right there. Because the frogs of Aotearoa New Zealand, the pepeketua, don't fit the stereotype. The four species of New Zealand frogs (Hochstetter's, Archey's, Hamilton's and Maud Island frogs) belong right alongside the dinosaurs - they were around at the same time. And they are a wee bit different to most modern frogs. In fact, they've hardly changed in 70 million years. For a start, they have no ears (at least none that show). All that croaking from the three introduced frog species just passes them by.

So, what about tadpoles? Nope, pepeketua don't do tadpoles either. Instead, they hatch as nearly fully formed small adults. Pepeketua childcare is pretty good, too, compared to leaving tadpoles to fend for themselves in a pond - in the case of Archey's frogs, the dad carries his children on his back until they are ready to go out in the world on their own.

Alright, what about hanging out in ponds? Well, sort-of. All NZ frogs need a moist habitat. But they usually plump for moist forests instead of ponds. The one exception is Hochstetter's frog, the most common native frog. It's happiest streamside, and has partially webbed feet - the other three don't have webbed feet because they don't need them in the forest.

So, are they green? Sometimes. A bit. Actually, they tend to brown, but Archey's frogs can have splashes of green and red as well. All of them are really well camouflaged.

SCIENCE AND SONG

One of the most unusual things about our sadly rare and endangered native frogs is that they have leftover tail-wagging muscles! I wonder if they miss wagging their lost tadpole tails?

One thing that native New Zealand frogs share with other frogs is a sensitivity to pollution and habitat change. They can also be badly affected by amphibian chytrid fungus (said 'ki-trid'), which has killed frogs all over the world.

ACTIVITY

Discovery Activity: Find out what frogs live near you. Do they make sounds? And if they do, do they croak all year round, or just some of the time? Frogs are often nocturnal, so if you want to hear them you might have to listen at night. But do native frogs a favour – don't go into their habitat, or if you do, make sure everything you are wearing starts off clean, even your shoes. Save your puddle-jumping for places without NZ native frogs!

SING FOR THE EARTH - LITTLE WILD ANIMALS

PANDA ON A PLANE

Bei Bei (Bei Bei) bye bye (bye bye)
Panda flying on a plane
Bei Bei (Bei Bei) bye bye (bye bye)
Up up up up up away
Bei Bei (Bei Bei) bye bye (bye bye)
Panda growing tall, off to see some more
Of the world (up up up up away)
So climb aboard

Bei Bei (Bei Bei) bye bye (bye bye)
Where you wanna go today?
Bei Bei (Bei Bei) bye bye (bye bye)
Up up up up away
Bei Bei (Bei Bei) bye bye (bye bye)
Heading for the sky, time to fly above
All the clouds (Up up up up up away)

SCIENCE AND SONG

So let's head out
Up up up up up up away

Bei Bei (Bei Bei) ni hao (ni hao)
Panda flying in the plane
Bei Bei (Bei Bei) ni hao ni hao
To the motherland again
Bei Bei (Bei Bei) ni hao (ni hao)
Panda growing strong
Back to find the place you belong
(up up up up away)
So let's head on
Up up up up up away

Bei Bei Bei Bei
Panda flying on a plane
Bei Bei Bei Bei
Panda flying on a plane
Ohhh, up up up up up up up away

(C) Claudia Robin Gunn, 2022

FIND OUT

WORLD-TRAVELLING PANDA

Giant panda are one of the most recognised animals in the world, their distinctive black and white coats making them easy to recognise, their bamboo-munching habits well-known. But the panda is under threat, with only around 2000 panda living in the wild. They are slow breeders, and have some unusual features that make it hard for them to breed in captivity.

They breed just once a year, the females are fertile (that is, can become pregnant) for just over one day a year, and they're very choosy about who they mate with. Their babies are born tiny and helpless (and pink, not black and white), and need to be looked after by their mothers for two years after they are born. Panda mothers hold their babies in their paws at first – panda babies can't walk for their first three months of life.

Captive breeding programs have only been successful relatively recently, though their success rate has improved, and panda have now been born in zoos around the world. There are large panda research programs in China, which have helped more pandas to breed in captivity. Pandas in captivity often have twins; in the wild, one twin would die, but in captivity both can be kept alive.

Captive breeding efforts mean that there are now about 600 panda in captivity, in addition to those in the wild. But panda are only released into the wild at 2 years of age (when they would naturally leave their mothers), and only a few are released in any year because of the huge effort that reintroduction takes. People involved in the reintroduction programs wear panda suits around the panda cubs, so that they won't become used to humans.

The word for a group of panda is an embarrassment!

Giant panda are loaned to countries outside China for up to ten years, for a yearly fee. But any panda born outside China has to be returned to China after 4 years, boarding a plane to return to their unseen homeland, where they will take part in the breeding programs. Most panda born in captivity stay there.

However, the biggest threat for giant panda is habitat loss. Like other large *mammals*, they need large areas in which to make their homes. Development and fragmentation of the bamboo forests where they live make them vulnerable. They also face threats from climate change, which affects which bamboos grow (panda need to eat up to 48 different varieties of bamboo).

Despite bamboo planting programs and reserves for panda being established in their home range, panda habitat remains fragmented, making it difficult for wild panda to safely move around in order to find food or mates (they can be hit by cars, or come into conflict with humans). Although they are no longer endangered, giant panda still face a hard road ahead, and a lot of plane journeys.

Costume Activity: Dress up as a panda! You could use face paint to give yourself the classic panda eyes, make yourself a mask, or go all out with a panda onesie if you have one.

SING FOR THE EARTH - LITTLE WILD ANIMALS

PEKAPEKA PUKAPUKA
(NZ Bat)

Pekapeka rere ahiahi

Didn't see 'em anywhere, didn't hear anything
Didn't even know their name
Here on this island, in the ocean
At the bottom of a planet in space

But then I took a little listening bug
That senses the frequencies
I went to find out where these little tiny fluffy hidey
Creatures of the night might be

All the pekapeka, pekapeka

The tiny mammals of our land
They are the pekapeka, pekapeka
Smaller than my little hand

SCIENCE AND SONG

Pekapeka rere ahiahi
Pekapeka rere ahiahi

You mightn't see them, you might not hear them
But they're part and parcel of this place
Here on our island in the ocean
At the bottom of a planet in space

Will you take a little listening bug
To gather all the frequencies?
And try and find out where the little tiny fluffy hidey
Creatures of the night might be

Meet the pekapeka, pekapeka
In the hollows of the oldest trees
All the pekapeka, pekapeka
Tiny mammals flying free
This is the pekapeka pukapuka
So everybody can lend a hand
It's the pekapeka pukapuka
All about the tiny mammals of this land

Pekapeka rere ahiahi
Pekapeka rere ahiahi
Pekapeka rere ahiahi
Pekapeka rere ahiahi

(C) Claudia Robin Gunn, 2022

PLAY SONGS

A BIT ABOUT BATS

The pekapeka is New Zealand's only land mammal. In fact, the pekapeka is the name for New Zealand's only *two* land mammals: the short-tailed bat and the long-tailed bat.

The long-tailed bat, pekapeka tou-roa, is a cute wee thing weighing only 10 grams - about the same as two sugar cubes. It's most often seen flying along the edges of forests and near waterways at dusk, searching for tasty moths. It's not too fussy though. Pekapeka tou-roa will eat pretty much any flying insect they can catch, including mosquitoes and midges, hunting by echolocation (high-pitched squeaks about 40 kilohertz, much too high for humans to hear).

These bats live in roosts in old trees, where they find crevices and holes to squeeze into. They usually have many different roosts, moving from tree to tree as they see fit. No-one really knows why they move so often, but it makes them quite difficult to count. It also means they need lots of big old trees to survive, so protecting old forest is really important for pekapeka. Since people started looking for bats in Aotearoa New Zealand, small groups of them have been found in lots of unexpected places.

The other pekapeka (the short-tailed bat) also needs lots of forest to live in. But the short-tailed bat uses its wings to fly to the forest floor, where it crawls around looking for food and using its wings like legs! It eats fruits and pollen as well as insects. It is very vulnerable to predators like cats, rats and stoats, due to its method of hunting for food.

SCIENCE AND SONG

Pekapeka tou-roa is associated in Māori legend with the hōkioi, a mythical night-flying bird signifying disaster (although some versions suggest that the proverb "pekapeka rere ahiahi, hōkioi rere pō" is meant to hasten travellers home, since the bat flies at twilight, before nightfall).

Citizen science activity: Join a bat walk! Quite a few organizations arrange bat walks in summer. These walks are done with 'bat boxes' along to locate bats by their echolocation. You can even borrow bat boxes from some councils, and do your own bat walk. If you do hear a bat, make sure you report it, to the Department of Conservation or to your local council. If there are no bat boxes available near you, try taking your family to sit quietly near a pond with old trees around it at dusk. You never know: you might just spot a pekapeka.

PINK FLAMINGO FLING

The pink flamingo fling

Meet Marina Maraschino, the stretchy pink flamingo
She leads the pink flamingo wing display
All the other pink flamingos, follow her where she goes
And do their level best to keep the pace
Outstretched go her wings for a second
See her black flying feathers underneath
And the rest stretch their wings out wide
Then they fold them back just in time for tea

It's the pink flamingo fling
It's the pink flamingo fling
It's the pink flamingo fling we can all join in
Cos flamingos are a merry kind of band

The pink flamingo fling

SCIENCE AND SONG

Meet Concertina Charlie, the daring pink flamingo
He directs the marchers as they turn
So many pink flamingos, putting on a marching show
This way, that way and return
To the left - to the right
Pink flamingos in sync as they follow
Concertina and the band, all the pink flamingo fans
Heads high, legs stride

It's the pink flamingo fling
It's the pink flamingo fling
It's the pink flamingo fling we can all join in
Cos flamingos are a merry kind of band

Meet Valentina Vita the calmest of flamingos
Balancing on one long leg with ease
It's a simple kind of style, can you hold it for a while?
Pink flamingo yoga is a breeze

Pink flamingos

Meet Ballerina Bindi, the little grey flaminglet
Fluffy feathers shiver as she points pink feet
Little grey flaminglets, copy all her dance steps
First, second, third, point, twirl then repeat!

It's the pink flamingo fling
It's the pink flamingo fling
It's the pink flamingo fling
We can all join in
Cos flamingos are a merry kind of band
Everybody
Flamingos are a merry kind of band
All together
Flamingos are a merry kinda band
Pink flamingos (repeat x8)

(C) Claudia Robin Gunn, 2022

FLAMINGO FLING

Everyone knows flamingos - big pink birds with super-long necks and legs. Did you know that adult flamingos are pink through and through? Even their blood is pink! But their pinkness depends on what they eat; they need enough of a chemical called carotene to stay pink. Carotene is found in the plant and animal plankton which flamingo eat. They sieve their food from shallow water using their unique beaks upside-down. The only flamingos that aren't pink are babies, which start off greyish, and birds which are unwell (or kept in zoos with less carotene in their diet).

There are six different species of flamingo: Three in South America, one in the Caribbean, and two in Africa, Europe and Asia. There are even extinct flamingos in Australia.

Flamingos liked to mingle! They're usually found in large flocks, sometimes containing thousands of individuals. When breeding time comes around, the large flock splits up into smaller groups. These groups perform breeding displays where all birds move at once in a complicated courtship dance - the flamingo fling! They walk to and fro, heads held high, or flicking rapidly from side to side. They dip and dance, and flap their wings.

While they're in breeding mode, they build mud nest platforms on a suitable mudflat. Both males and females contribute to defending the nest, egg and chick. A really interesting aspect of flamingos is that male and female both feed the chick crop milk produced from glands in their digestive tract.

After two weeks of being fed by their parents, flamingo chicks are herded into small groups called microcrèches, where they are left alone. Later, they form larger crèches with thousands of other chicks, filtering food from silty water like their parents. The large numbers help protect them from predators.

Dance Activity: Gather some friends or classmates and make up a choreographed group dance. Try using some flamingo moves! Everyone could turn their heads in one direction at the same time, or come up with some fancy footwork.

SING FOR THE EARTH - LITTLE WILD ANIMALS

RAINBOW WORLD
(BIODIVERSITY)

We live in a rainbow world

How do you feel yellow bee?
What will you play blue spotted ray?
What will you sing black swallow?
What will you think of tomorrow?
What can you see green parrot?
What can you smell brown bear?
What can you hear grey elephant
Under the rainbow shining here?

If I had wings or a beak or could walk on four feet
Or had flippers and gills or a lizards fine frills
Would I love sunshine or would I seek shadows?
Would I see more colours in every rainbow?
Would I be able to walk in their shoes
And know that these colours are too good to lose?

SCIENCE AND SONG

What do you know shiny stone?
What do you see tallest tree?
Why do you ripple, running river?
And what do you dream of?
Do you remember, great mountains
When you were down there below?
And where do you rush to so slow,
oh glacier all covered in snow?

Do you love sunshine or do you seek shadows?
Do you see more colours in every rainbow?
If I was able to walk in your shoes
Would I know that this world is much too good to lose?

So show me your colours
World show me your colours

Yellow bee, blue ray, black swallow,
will I see you tomorrow?
Green parrot, brown bear, grey elephant
What do you hear oh what do you hear?
Shiny stone, tallest tree running river
what is in your heart?
Great mountains, glaciers remember

We live in a rainbow world
So show me your colours
World show me your colours
So show me your colours
World show me your colours
(show me your colours)
Don't lose your colours, oh
We live in a rainbow world

(C) Claudia Robin Gunn, 2022

SING FOR THE EARTH - LITTLE WILD ANIMALS

FIND OUT: BIODIVERSITY: A RAINBOW WORLD

Biodiversity is all life on earth – everything living, in an infinite rainbow of animals, birds, insects, plants, even bacteria, and everything in between. Over one and a half million species (types of living thing) have been documented, but there are probably many more. New species are being found all the time.

At the moment, biodiversity is being lost – and that's a problem, because we live in an intricate web, where every living thing depends on another. There are lots of videos about why biodiversity is important – David Attenborough is the most famous producer, but there are many more.

Luckily, there are things we can do to help reduce biodiversity loss, even at home. Reducing plastic pollution helps. So do actions like making bug hotels in your backyard, or leaving your lawn unmown to provide more flowers for pollinators like bees. Find out what variety of creatures make their home in your backyard, and learn about them. Plant a garden. Go on nature walks. Join a bio-blitz, where experts can help you identify all the organisms in a small area. Spend time outdoors and observe!

Activity: Draw a web of life! For example, plants get energy from the sun. Snails get energy by eating the plants. Birds get energy by eating the snails. Draw a picture of the sun, some plants, some animals that eat plants, maybe even some animals that eat animals, and draw lines between each of them showing the flow of energy. Then consider if there are any other links between the animals you have drawn. Maybe the snails eat more than one type of plant. Maybe aphids also eat the plants, and spiders catch the aphids, ants feed the aphids, and birds also feed on the aphids. Some birds also pollinate plants (like feijoas), so the plants need the birds, too. See how many links you can think of!

You can find an example of this game here: https://www.sciencelearn.org.nz/resources/1526-making-a-food-web

SING FOR THE EARTH - LITTLE WILD ANIMALS

LYRICS
ROLY POLY POLAR BEAR

Hello little roly poly polar bear
In your light reflecting warm collecting
Mama's waiting best be hasty snow white fur
In the Arctic snow on the ice
you'll swim and dive and catch
And run and sleep and roly poly grow

Show show me your little roly poly baby twinkle toes
Stomp stomp stomp
Your little roly polar bear feet
Wriggle like an otter, swim like a fish
Slide like a penguin, splash splash splish
In the Arctic snow by the sea
you'll swim and dive and catch
And run and sleep and roly poly grow

If the sea ice melts, when the hot sun glows
Where will little roly poly baby polar bears
and their parents go?

Oh such a dear little roly poly polar bear
In your light reflecting warm collecting
Mama's waiting best be hasty snow white fur
You still need somewhere cold to swim and dive and catch
And run and sleep and roly poly grow
By the sea you'll swim and dive and catch
And run and sleep and roly poly grow
On the ice you'll swim and dive and catch
And run and sleep and roly poly grow
Little roly poly polar bear in your polar bear home

If the sea ice melts, when the hot sun glows
Where will little roly poly baby polar bears
and their parents go?

Oh such a dear little roly poly polar bear
In your light reflecting warm collecting
Mama's waiting best be hasty snow white fur
You still need somewhere cold to swim and dive and catch
And run and sleep and roly poly grow

By the sea you'll swim and dive and catch
And run and sleep and roly poly grow
On the ice you'll swim and dive and catch
And run and sleep and roly poly grow
Little roly poly polar bear in your polar bear home

(C) Claudia Robin Gunn, 2022

BIG-PAWED POLAR BEARS

Polar bears, sometimes called ice-bears, are the largest living land carnivore. However, they depend on sea-ice to hunt their preferred prey of seals, and as such are actually marine mammals. They are the biggest bear species, and they have many adaptations to enable them to survive in ice and snow. Polar bears have small ears, big feet, a short snout and short legs, plus two layers of dense fur, and a layer of fat which helps to keep them warm. They really are roly poly.

The way they keep their roly poly nature is to eat fat, lots of fat. In fact, when adult polar bears eat seals, they mostly eat the blubber, not the meat. That way, they don't have to pee much (because peeing loses heat!). Most animals wouldn't be able to survive on a diet with so much fat in it. But polar bears thrive. That's because of some special internal adaptations which enable them to process fat straight into fat cells.

Polar bears sometimes see people as snacks, so finding polar bear paw prints is good (because that means there are polar bears) and bad (because that means you need to be careful of polar bears). Their front and back paws are different shapes, just as our handprints are different from our footprints.

It's the polar bears' need for sea-ice that is now a problem for them. Climate change means that there is less sea-ice every year. Without sea-ice, polar bears struggle to catch seals, which makes them less than roly-poly. The adaptations they have to enable them to survive in the ice and snow mean that they can't cope with warmer conditions. They get too hot really fast.

Because of the pace of climate change it is unlikely that polar bears can adapt fast enough to thrive in a warmer world, although some may interbreed with their distant grizzly bear cousins to form a more heat-tolerant hybrid. The best hope for polar bears is for people to make dramatic changes in our lifestyles, to stop climate change from getting worse.

ACTIVITY

Measuring activity: Measure your footprint and compare it to a polar bear print! Get a felt tip pen or a pencil, a big piece of paper, and a 30cm ruler. Using your pen or pencil, trace around your foot on the paper. Now take a ruler and measure how long your footprint is. After that, line up the ruler lengthways along your footprint. Draw a 30cm line. Then move the ruler so it's in the middle of that line (at 15 cm) and draw a 20 cm perpendicular line (across your footprint). Use the two lines to draw a bear's paw print. That's about how big a polar bear print can be! Compare the bear print and your footprint. Which is bigger?

Action activity: Though a polar bear paw print would be WAY bigger than a kid's footprint, when it comes to carbon footprints, sadly the opposite is likely the case. Find out what your family can do to reduce your carbon footprint (that's an estimate of how much carbon dioxide you release into the atmosphere). There are handy online calculators to help you do this.

Here's a New Zealand one: https://www.futurefit.nz/

SING FOR THE EARTH - LITTLE WILD ANIMALS

TARA TUATARA

Tara tuatara told me a story just the other day
About how the world is warming;
it's not good for tuatara babies

She said the time was short but the years are long
We can find a way (come on people)
Cos we are the living fossils
Survivors of the dinosaur age

We only live on the islands now;
we used to be everywhere
We are the kings and queens of an island kingdom
and ocean air (come on people)

You know the time is short but the years are long
And we can find a way (come on people)
We are the living fossils
Survivors of the dinosaur age

Tara tuatara blinked her third eye
and told me what she saw
Tara tuatara wanted to warn us what we had in store
(come on people)

SCIENCE AND SONG

She said the time was short but the years are long
And we can find a way (come on people)
We are the living fossils
Survivors of the dinosaur age

The order sphenodontia needs a little help today
We are the living fossils
Survivors of the dinosaur age

Come on people
Come on people
Come on people
Come on people
Come on people, come on people
Come on people cool things down
Come on people, come on people
Come on people cool things down
For Tara tuatara and all her tuatara babies

(C) Claudia Robin Gunn, 2022

SURVIVOR OF THE DINOSAUR AGE

Tuatara are reptiles, but very unique ones. Although they resemble lizards, they are the last surviving members of an order of animals, *Rhynchocephalia*, that was widespread in the time of the dinosaurs. The other Rhynchocephalia went extinct 60 million years ago, leaving only the tuatara. They are only found in New Zealand, and they're really quite odd.

Tuatara means 'peaks on the back', a name which refers to the spines that run down their back. Their teeth are fused to their jawbone, and they chew their meals. Tuatara are most active at night, when they hunt insects, spiders, lizards, the eggs of burrow-nesting seabirds and even young tuatara! During the day they are happy to bask in the sun, almost motionless - but they can move fast if a wētā or other tasty morsel happens by. Tuatara can live to be over 100 years old.

Tuatara also have a 'third eye'. Rather than a true eye, this is a patch of light-sensitive tissue (see-through in juveniles), which is gradually covered with scales. Scientists aren't sure of the function of this light-sensitive patch.

Tuatara used to be found all over New Zealand, but they disappeared from the mainland a long time ago, surviving on offshore islands. Recent studies found that they breed successfully only when rats are removed from their habitat, suggesting that rats are eating the eggs or young tuatara.

Tuatara also been bred in captivity, which has led to some fascinating discoveries. Tuatara are adapted for life in relatively low temperatures - although they enjoy sunbathing, they don't thrive if the temperature is constantly over 25°C. Unusually for reptiles, they can be active in temperatures as low as 6°C.

Even more importantly, the sex of their offspring is determined by temperature. When tuatara eggs are incubated below 22°C, they hatch as females. However, when the temperature of incubation is higher, they hatch as males. This is important for conservation efforts, because as the global temperature increases, more tuatara will hatch as males. Tuatara need cool weather!

Action activity: Do your own back-yard pest monitoring! You can use tracking tunnels to see what predators you have in your back yard. Make a tunnel using recycled materials such as old milk bottles, with the tops and bottoms cut off to make a tunnel. Place a piece of white paper on the bottom of your tunnel, then cut two pieces of sponge that are wide enough to cover the bottom of the tunnel. Drop some food colouring into the pieces of sponge. Leave paper showing on either side of the sponge, and a small space in the middle of the tunnel. Put a teaspoon of peanut butter in that space, then place your tunnel outside overnight. When animals walk into the tunnel to eat the peanut butter, they have to walk on the sponge. Their footprints will then make prints on the paper. You can figure out which animals have visited your tunnel using the information on the Department of Conservation's website:

https://www.doc.govt.nz/Documents/our-work/predator-free-2050/a-short-guide-to-identifying-footprints-on-tracking-tunnel-papers.pdf

There are more detailed instructions for building a tracking tunnel from **KCC** here: https://kcc.org.nz/portfolio/make-a-tracking-tunnel/

SING FOR THE EARTH - LITTLE WILD ANIMALS

THE LITTLE BLUE SUSHI SHOP PENGUINS

Underneath the sushi shop
First there came a little squark
Then there came an answer from the harbour
The sushi chefs were busy, rolling up the sushi
When they heard the noise they stopped
Oh fish - what's that?

And the little blue sushi shop penguins
Were hiding underneath of the air vents
The little blue sushi shop penguins
Were looking for nice warm place to call their home
Oh no!

So they lured them out with fish
Shut them in the sushi fridge
Til the city officers arrived
"You can't stay here" the officers say
"We usually give tickets but not today
Dear little penguins - run back to the bay!"

SCIENCE AND SONG

And the little blue sushi shop penguins
Were hiding underneath of the air vents
The little blue sushi shop penguins
Were looking for nice warm place to call their home
Oh no!

Now in the middle of Lambton Quay
Little and blue and brave can be
Holding up the traffic as they waddled
Oh on the way to the sushi shop
"This is the place we like a lot
Commuting distance from the sea
- it's the perfect place for me!"

And the little blue sushi shop penguins
Were hiding underneath of the air vents
The little blue sushi shop penguins
Were looking for nice warm place to call their home
Oh no!

Two days later they both came back
"Haven't we warned you already bout that?"
The officers were pulling out their hair!
"We know you need a nesting spot
Underneath a sushi shop
Isn't the best real estate
You can better down by the bay"
"Oh good idea"

Now the little blue sushi shop penguins
Are cosy inside their rocky nest
The little blue sushi shop penguins
Have a nice warm safe cosy place to call their home
Good show!

(C) Claudia Robin Gunn, 2022

LITTLE BLUE PENGUINS

The southern regions of Oceania (in other words, Australia and New Zealand - the other countries of Oceania are further north) are home to the little penguin - known as the fairy penguin in Australia, kororā in te reo Māori in New Zealand, and also as the little blue penguin. As you can guess by the last name, the feathers on this small penguin's back are blue. It's the smallest of all living penguins.

Unlike the movie-star penguins which live in Antarctica, far from people and their boats, cars and pets, little penguins like to live in the same place as a lot of people - on the coast, in nice warm places (but not too warm). They spend their days fishing not too far from the beach, and come ashore at night. They prepare their nests in burrows or rocky crevices, up to 300 metres inland. They also moult on land. That means that people and penguins can come into contact - though penguins don't like being disturbed.

More houses built near the coast means less places for penguins to nest (unless the penguins choose to nest *under* your house), and more dogs and cats around. So if you live near the coast, or are visiting, it's a good idea to keep cats indoors at night, and keep dogs on a leash when out and about, just in case there are penguins nearby. You can help by making sure there is predator control to reduce rats, mice and stoats around penguin habitat. Look out for them on coastal roads, too! Penguins often have to cross roads to reach their nests.

Online Activity: Watch a little blue penguin livestream! Here's one to try from Oamaru: https://www.penguins.co.nz/

The West Coast Penguin Trust has published a whole book of penguin-related activites. Have a look here:

https://www.westcoastpenguintrust.org.nz/projects/education/

Exploration activity: Go to the beach and look for penguin prints. If you have a dog, keep it on a leash while you do this.

Measuring activity: Little blue penguins eat about 25% (a quarter (1/4)) of their body weight every day, usually small fish, crustaceans or squid. Weigh yourself on some scales and work out how much food you would have to eat if you were a penguin.

SING FOR THE EARTH - LITTLE WILD ANIMALS

THE VERY BUSY SLOTH

I'm a sloth but I'm not just lazing around
Up here in the trees so far off the ground
I eat green leaves and I chew them slow
I don't get dizzy upside down you know

I'm thinking my way through a million things
My brain works so fast I get giddy
So I may look like I'm doing nothing at all
But really I'm actually quite busy

(I'm a sloth)
I have three toes, some sloth have two
On humans you'd call them fingers
(I'm a sloth)
I've a very long tongue, long claws, green fur
It gets covered in algae, I don't mind - it's tasty

SCIENCE AND SONG

And I'm thinking my way through a trillion things
My brain works so fast I get giddy
So I may look like I'm doing nothing at all
But really I'm actually quite busy

(I'm a sloth)
Back in the olden days we were much bigger
We were called megatherium
Giant sloth as large as an elephant
Can you even imagine?

Now I'm thinking my way through gazillions of things
My brain works so fast I get giddy
And I may look like I'm doing nothing at all
Really I'm actually quite busy

I'm a sloth but I'm not just lazing around
Up here in the trees so far off the ground

(I'm a sloth)
Thinking my way through gazillion things
(I'm a sloth)
Thinking my way through a trillion things
(I'm a sloth)
Thinking my way through a million things
(I'm a sloth)
Don't tell me I don't look busy
Oh no no Oh no no

(C) Claudia Robin Gunn, 2022

SING FOR THE EARTH - LITTLE WILD ANIMALS

SLOTH TIME: SLOW TIME

Sloths are *really* slow. They might actually be the slowest-moving land mammals around. Even their name means slow, or lazy. Sloths themselves aren't lazy, though - they move at just the right speed to avoid being spotted by predators like jaguar or eagles, which tend to find their prey by watching for movement.

They also avoid being spotted by growing their own green camouflage: algae! Sloths grow algae in their fur, which gives them a green appearance - perfect for blending into the leaves of their tree-top habitats. Their algae-covered fur hosts a whole mini-ecosystem of insects, including sloth moths, some of which occur nowhere else. Sloth fur grows in the opposite direction to most animals, facing towards their head rather than away from it. No-one's quite sure of the reason for this, though there are plenty of theories.

Sloths spend a lot of time hanging around in trees - they have specially adapted claws which make it easy for them to do this. They eat in trees, sleep in trees, and even give birth in trees! Just about the only time sloths come out of their trees is when they need to go to the toilet, about once a week. Some scientists think that the sloth moths take that chance to lay their eggs.

There are two-toed and three-toed sloths. Three-toed sloths move a bit slower, and eat mostly leaves, while the two-toed sloths' diet is a bit more varied. Leaves are low in energy and take a long time to digest, especially since some of them contain poisons that need to be processed slowly. That's probably why sloths spend three quarters of their life asleep!

They also have a really low body temperature - at about 34 degrees C, they're much colder than humans. They warm themselves up or cool off by moving in and out of sunlight, a bit like reptiles.

On land, sloths move about 3 metres a minute. But there's one place that sloths can move fast: in the water. With their long front legs, sloths can swim a lot faster than they can walk. When necessary - to find a mate, or to find food - they can swim for it. There's even fossil evidence for an aquatic sloth (one that lived in the water!).

Sloths can see in colour, but their hearing and eyesight is pretty poor. That means they find their food by smell and touch more than by sight. Luckily, leaves don't move fast either. Sloths have great spatial memory (knowing what is where), based on smell, sound and touch. They're pretty smart that way.

Activity: Have a slow race! People sometimes live life in the fast lane. This activity will help you slow down. With a friend or two, or a parent if you can persuade them to slow down, see how long you can take to go three metres. Measure the distance, or get someone to measure it for you. Get a timer, set it going, and you're off! Can you do it slower than a sloth? (you have to be moving the whole time, mind you - no sneaky naps on the racecourse).

SING FOR THE EARTH - LITTLE WILD ANIMALS

LYRICS
THIS BOOK BELONGS TO EVERYONE

This book is history
This book everything in you and me
This book belongs to everyone
This book belongs to everyone
This book is as old as the universe
As young as a baby born this minute

This book is the story of all of us
The story that we all write
Everyone gets their name in the action
The footnotes, the inlays, the margins
Full colour plates mixed with black and white sketches
From the minute to the infinite experience

SCIENCE AND SONG

This is the book of the creatures and the bones
Their DNA and traces fossilised in limestone
This is the book - the record in the rings
Of the weather back then, and did the songbirds sing?
This is the book of the creatures and the bones
Their DNA and traces fossilised in limestone

This is the book of life
Oh the story that we all write
This book belongs to everyone
(This book is history)
This book belongs to everyone
(This book is everything in you and me)
This book belongs to everyone
This book belongs to everyone

(C) Claudia Robin Gunn, 2022

THE BOOK OF EVERYTHING (DNA)

You might have heard of **DNA** (deoxyribonucleic acid, if you want the whole mouthful of a word!). You might even know that **DNA** (or in some viruses, **RNA**) provides the codes that tell our bodies how to grow, what colour our hair will be, and what colour our eyes will be. Alright, viruses don't have hair. But did you know that scientists can use **DNA** to tell a whole lot more? Different types of **DNA** are used for different purposes.

Scientists can use **eDNA** (DNA found in the environment, for example in dirt or in streams) to find out what animals are in an area, without even seeing them. **eDNA** can't (yet) tell us much about what individual animals are like. **DNA** samples taken directly from animals or plants can be used to find out information such as who the individual's parents might be, or how closely related they are to others in the neighbourhood.

But it doesn't stop there. **DNA** holds our history! Using the right tools, scientists can investigate the deep past, finding out not just who our ancestors were, but also who their ancestors were, and even what happened to them as a group — if there were lots of them or only a few, and where they might have come from.

There's a ton of information coiled up tight in the double helix that is **DNA**. Some **DNA** is only passed down by mothers (**mtDNA**, also known as mitochondrial **DNA**). Some is only passed down by fathers. Some **DNA** is borrowed from bacteria or even viruses, like the genes that make up the A-B-O blood types! It all goes into the mix and can tell us things. It's a book we're beginning to be able to read, the book of life.

We can combine information from DNA with other evidence of what happened in the past to form a story that makes sense. For example, we can count and measure tree rings to find out what was happening to the climate in a particular year or series of years, and match that with what was happening to a population based on its DNA.

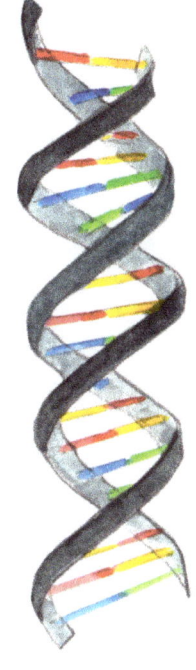

Activity: Make a DNA double helix model. You'll need some beads in 4 colours, and 4 pipe cleaners. Cut two of the pipe cleaners into short strips - about 5cm long. String two beads onto each short strip, making sure there's some pipe cleaner free at each end. Next, string beads onto the two long pipe cleaners. Once you've done that, twist the free ends of each short beaded pipe cleaner strip around the two long pipe cleaners, like a ladder. Finally, give your ladder a twist or two. You now have a double helix!

Advanced activity: Make a DNA helix with origami! Follow the instructions here:

https://www.stem.org.uk/elibrary/resource/29637

OR make up a code based on the bead colours you have chosen. Can you code short words into your helix?

SING FOR THE EARTH - LITTLE WILD ANIMALS

WE ARE THE PLATYPUS

Poisonous talons, swim with our eyes closed
Electromagnetic senses in our nose
Burrows in the river banks, two layers of fur
Bill like a duck, swim like a fish
Do you know who we are?

Semi aquatic egg laying mammals
Furry like an otter, paddle shaped tail
We only eat meat not plants
Cos we're carnivores
Watch out beetles and swimming snails
Cicadas and shrimp and tadpoles tails

We are the platypus
We are not a curiosity
We are just the only living ones of our kind
We're quite mysterious
We're platypus

Mammals that lay eggs are quite unusual
Platypus babies - we are called puggles
Underneath the water our fur can glow
Why on earth this happens - no one knows

We're platypus
We are the platypus
We are not a curiosity
We are just the only living ones of our kind
We're quite mysterious
We're are the platypus
We're are the platypus
We're are the platypus
We're quite mysterious

(C) Claudia Robin Gunn, 2022

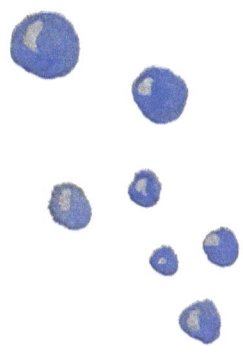

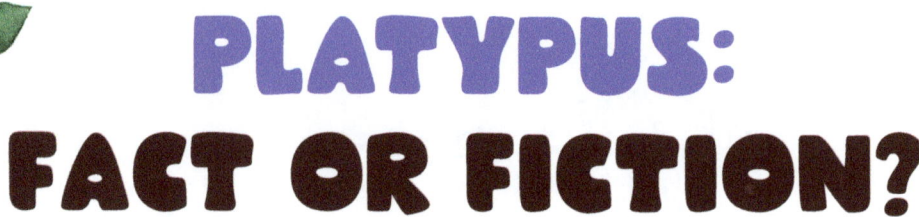

PLATYPUS: FACT OR FICTION?

When platypus were first seen by European scientists, they thought it was a practical joke made of many different animals. With its duck-like bill, beaver-like tail and otter-like webbed feet, the platypus seemed like a chimera (said 'ki-mee-ra') – a mix of parts. Of course, it wasn't a joke, but it was and is one of the most unusual mammals on Earth.

As you would expect from its webbed feet, it lives a semi-aquatic lifestyle, spending up to 12 hours a day diving for food – though each dive only lasts 30 seconds or so. The way it finds the insects, shrimps and yabbies (freshwater crayfish) that make up its diet is also unusual for a mammal: it closes its white-lidded eyes and swims blind, using sensors in its bill to detect pressure and to electrolocate its prey. That means it senses the tiny electrical signatures of living things!

When not hunting, platypus retreat to their riverside burrows, so as to avoid the hawks, eagles, dingos, or even crocodiles that would otherwise prey on them. Females do another unlikely thing in their burrows: they lay eggs. Platypus are in the monotreme group of mammals, which are the only mammals to lay eggs. Like any other mammal, they feed their babies milk, but their milk seeps through pores in their skin so that their young can lap it up.

The surprises don't end there: the platypus glows blue-green in the dark! (though only if people shine ultraviolet light on them). They are also one of the only venomous *mammals*; males have a hind-leg spur connected to a venomous gland.

As if all that weren't enough, platypuses store fat in their tail, and also share some of their DNA with birds.

Drawing Activity: Use your imagination to invent your own mixed up animal - a chimera. Draw it! Can you make it more unusual than a platypus? Sometimes fact is stranger than fiction.

Bonus Activity: Mystery bag. Identify objects using only your sense of touch. Get a friend to put a few things in a bag, close your eyes, put your hand in the bag and guess what you're feeling. Keep it fair, and have your friend take the next turn guessing what's in the bag.

SING FOR THE EARTH - LITTLE WILD ANIMALS

ZOO HULLABALOO

It's the zoo hullaballoo
Come and sing with us too

Waiata, pakipaki, takahia, tārere
Hurihuri, kanikani
All together, tātou katoa

Waiata, can you sing too?
Come and do the zoo hullabaloo
Waiata, waiata, sing like a korimako waiata
Sing sing sing sing sing sing waiata

Pakipaki, can you clap too?
Come and do the zoo hullabaloo
Pakipaki, pakipaki, clap like an otter pakipaki
Clap clap clap clap clap clap pakipaki

Takahia can you stomp too?
Come and do the zoo hullabaloo
Takahia, takahia, stomp like an elephant takahia
Stomp stomp stomp stomp stomp stomp takahia

SCIENCE AND SONG

Tārere can you swing too?
Come and do the zoo hullaballoo
Tārere tārere, swing like orang-utans tārere
Swing swing swing swing swing swing tārere

Hurihuri can you twirl too?
Come and do the zoo hullaballoo
Hurihuri, hurihuri, twirl like a fur seal hurihuri
Twirl twirl twirl twirl twirl twirl hurihuri

Kanikani, can you dance too?
Come and do the zoo hullaballoo
Kanikani, kanikani, dance like a cockatoo kanikani
Dance dance dance dance dance dance kanikani
All together, tātou katoa

Oooh can you do the zoo
Can you do the zoo
Can you do the zoo
Can you do the zoo hullaballoo?

(C) Claudia Robin Gunn, 2022

FIND OUT

ANIMAL DANCE AT THE ZOO

Some people like to say that only humans can dance. Many folkloric dances include dances that mimic animals. But if you look at the 'animal kingdom', there are many animals that also dance. Most of them dance for specific reasons, such as courtship dances - trying to attract a mate. Birds are wonderful examples of this, with some spectacular courtship dances, from the flamingo fling to the intricate and varied dances of birds of paradise. Sometimes birds will coordinate their dances with a 'vocal display' (also known as a song - although the sounds they make might not sound melodic to us).

Recent research in lyrebirds (an Australian native) showed that male lyrebirds can display different choreographies with different songs. Importantly, the scientists also showed that lyrebirds can sing without dancing, so the dancing is not required to make the sounds. In a nutshell, that means that humans are not alone in liking to make a song & dance!

There are some other species that might dance to a beat, and they're all 'vocal mimics', animals that learn using sound. Parrots fall into this category. So do some bats, dolphins, whales, and elephants.

Dance activity: Put on some music and dance like your favourite animal! Or better still, dance like several of your favourite animals. Try this in a group, and everyone can take turns calling out which animal to dance.

WHY SCIENCE AND SONG?

Thank you for taking time with some of the fascinating, unique and special creatures we have presented through science and song. We hope you liked discovering more about the amazing biodiversity in our world. If there is a creature that you think needs its own song, you could let us know and we could make one for you, or you could even write your own!

Experiencing empathy and learning about animals and ecosystems as children may be a powerful influence in the choices they grow up to make as adults. Research suggests that the first step for conservation of any animal is connection. We made this book to help you, dear reader, discover some of the amazing biodiversity in our world.

little wild MUSIC

SONGWRITER

Claudia Robin Gunn is a New Zealand songwriter, and founder of label Little Wild Music. She is a two time APRA award winner and Tūī recipient, with much of her work dialling into nature and conservation themes.

"I write music for anyone looking for a sense of wonder, fun and enchantment in music, and who, like me, are amazed by the incredible beauty that exists in this world if we only stop and listen."

Find all of Claudia's songwriting collections at: claudiarobingunn.com and littlewildmusic.com

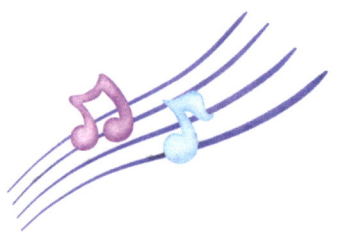

AUTHOR

Melissa R. Gunn brings her writing expertise (Imagine 2200 finalist) and scientific career (PhD in conservation genetics) to the task of creating written content that is both fun and meaningful, engaging and scientifically backed. Melissa has studied animals all over the world and is passionate about sharing her love of science and nature. She hopes to create links between kids, their families, and the wider conservation landscape, providing an access point from a STEM perspective to encourage families to gain a deeper understanding of their world.

Find out more about Melissa's writing projects at melissagunn.com

ARTIST

Award winning artist Elise De Silva brought a deft hand to the work of illustrating this project. In conversation with Claudia, Elise chose a mix of individual creatures and ecosystem worlds to highlight from the songs. Elise's sparkling watercolours encourage kids to adventure into the vibrant world of wildlife. Elise has illustrated 3 songbooks with Little Wild Music (this one, and also Sing Through the Year and Sing for the Sea). Elise is also an author, and teaches watercolour technique.

Find out more about Elise's magical art at elisedesilvaart.com

PRODUCER

After first picking up a guitar while growing up in South Africa, Tom Fox went on to become a session guitarist and award-winning music producer. Tom Fox is an audio engineer, songwriter and multi-instrumentalist. Tom and Claudia co-produced all the tracks with a sense of fun, exploration and musical curiosity, just like the amazing creatures who they have made these soundtracks for. Tom has produced many albums with Little Wild Music.

Find out more about Tom Fox at instagram.com/tomfoxnz

Additional illustrations were sourced from Envato elements, Creative Market and Depositphotos. No AI was used in the creation of this book.
This project was proudly supported by Creative New Zealand

creative nz
ARTS COUNCIL OF NEW ZEALAND TOI AOTEAROA

SING FOR THE EARTH - LITTLE WILD ANIMALS

we live in a RAINBOW WORLD
let's keep it that way

claudia robin gunn

www.ingramcontent.com/pod-product-compliance
Lightning Source LLC
Chambersburg PA
CBHW061158010526
44119CB00060B/857